Contents

Harry

Fred m. Wynn
Ballard

Frank

George m. Margaret

Freda

Bob

Peter m. Mary
Barlow (Grandma)

John

The Barlows
and
The Ballards

William m. Sara

Matthew
Barlow

Nicky
Barlow

1 Friends from Germany

Matthew Barlow ran up the garden path with his sister Nicky. "Hello, Grandma!" he shouted. "Is my rabbit OK?" But he hardly stopped for breath before telling Grandma about their holiday.

The Barlows had been staying in a caravan, close to the sea. "Swimming every day was great," explained Matthew. "I did some canoeing too. There was a German family staying in the next caravan – Benz came canoeing but he wasn't very good. His father's invited us to Germany next year. Have you ever been to Germany, Grandma?"

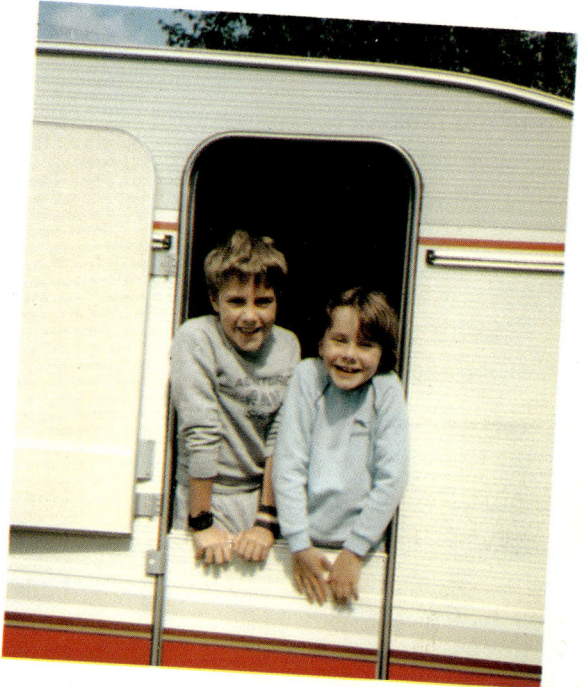

Matthew and Nicky on holiday

"Of course not," replied Grandma crossly. "Not after they tried to bomb me out of house and home forty years ago. For all you know, your friend's grandad could have been the bomber pilot!"

"But he couldn't have been," cried Matthew. "I saw his photo. He wasn't fierce. He looked just like Gramps, only older."

Matthew was upset that Grandma and Benz's grandad had been enemies. He tried to ask Grandma more about the war but she didn't want to answer.

"We'll talk about it another day," she said. "Now, who would like some cake?"

2 Grandma's treasures

The next Saturday, Matthew took his holiday photos round to show Grandma. She was pleased to see that he'd enjoyed himself but she still wasn't interested in his German friends.

"I'm sorry that my new friends have upset you, Grandma," said Matthew. "Was the war very bad for you?"

"It seemed so," replied Grandma. "The war changed everything. And there were times when we were very frightened. But it's difficult to remember anything clearly now. I was only young when the war started – a bit younger than Nicola."

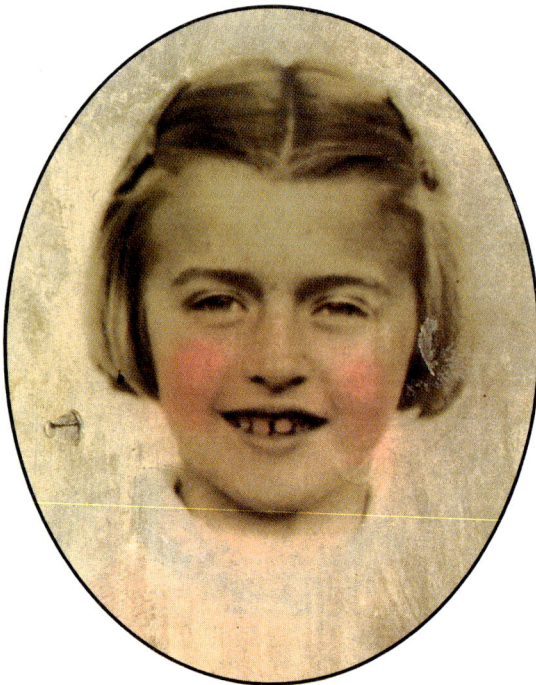

Grandma, aged 8

Matthew started laughing. "I can't imagine you as a little girl, Grandma," he said, so Grandma showed him a photograph of herself. "That's me when I was eight," she told him. "It was taken during the war."

Matthew couldn't imagine his Grandma in a real war. He read about war in his comics but the stories were always exciting, about fighting and winning medals. He couldn't imagine Grandma in one of those stories.

When he told Grandma this, she started laughing. "I'm afraid I don't know much about battles and guns," she said. "There wasn't any fighting in the streets of Great Yarmouth. But I can show you a few medals. They're in the sideboard with the photos."

For the next hour Matthew and Grandma searched through the sideboard. They hunted out the medals and laughed at the old-fashioned clothes in the photographs. By the time Nicky and Dad arrived, the floor was covered with Grandma's treasures. "Look at this, Dad!" shouted Matthew excitedly. "These medals belonged to my *great*-grandad. And Grandma kept these newspapers – there's a story about her in one of them. She's promised to tell me about it after tea. So hurry up, all of you."

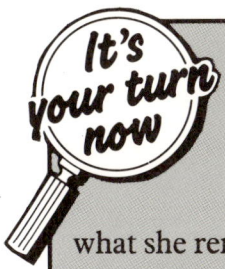

IMPLE, SMART AND SUITABLE

GIVE your "becoming shabby" suit a new little blouse and you will be surprised how it will sparkle up again. The one we picture above only takes one yard of material — two coupons — and how gay it would look in coral-pink linen-like fabric, worn with a grey suit. Simple machine - stitching is used for its adornment.
Allow 1 yard of 36-inch material.

ocks For "Off Duty" Hours d Aa Attractive Suit And ouse Cut From Short Lengths Of Material

(Left)
Bestway
Pattern No. 19,570.
Price 1/6 (by post 1/7).
Overseas 2/-.

(Left)
Bestway
Pattern No. 19,575.
Price 1/3 (by post 1/4).
Overseas 2/-.

(Left)
Bestway
Pattern No. 19,728.
Price 1/6 (by post 1/7).
Overseas 2/-.

IF you want to make yourself a suit but haven't any experience at tailoring, you should choose a "soft" or dressmaker style, such as No. 19,728. You will like its simple yet clever cutting lines and the skirt with the two slightly flared panels at front and the plain back. The coat has a centre back seam.
Allow 2½ or 2⅞ yards of 54-inch material.

PALESTINE

It's
your turn
now

Matthew was lucky. When he wanted to find out about life during the war, his Grandma could tell him what she remembered. She had also kept a lot of things from wartime. You can see them on these pages. What different types of things had Grandma kept?

3 A load of old rubbish?

After tea Grandma carefully opened one of the newspapers. "I still remember that day," she said, looking at the picture. "The boys kept fighting while the photographer was getting ready." Then she pointed to a girl almost hidden by a bedstead. "That's me," she said. "I was a bit shy. I hated knocking on the doors but I did my share of collecting."

"But why were you collecting old rubbish?" asked Matthew. So Grandma settled back and started to explain.

"During the war, there were always

What had Grandma's gang collected?

shortages. The government told us not to waste things – everything was collected and re-used. There were posters in the street, messages on the radio and advertisements in the papers. My mother said they even nagged her at the cinema.

At first, they only wanted us to collect aluminium, kettles and the like. One girl took her Mum's best saucepans to the collecting centre. She got into terrible trouble when her Mum found out.

MINISTRY OF SUPPLY

RUBBER SHORTAGE

GO EASY WITH YOUR TYRES

FAST DRIVING
WASTES RUBBER

90% of the world's natural rubber resources are in

TO ALL CAREFUL HOUSEWIVES

THANK YOU

"PAPER!

"METAL!

"BONES!

Put out bones, metal and paper. Put them out separately by your dustbin.
It's not always easy to remember that every scrap counts—but it's true. Every scrap *does* count. We've started well so keep it going—keep your friends interested—send suggestions to your local council. You are working for victory.

Advertisements from the *Daily Express* (13/8/1940) and the *Daily Mirror* (26/8/1942)

Later on, the government asked us to save almost everything. So a gang of us children, who were still at home, built a handcart and went from door to door collecting. We got tin cans, old jumpers, kitchen waste – it did seem like a load of old rubbish!

I remember collecting paper most of all – newspapers, books and letters. But I don't know what happened to it. There was never any wrapping paper in the shops. And my grandfather complained when the newspapers got thinner and thinner."

Another garden loses its gates

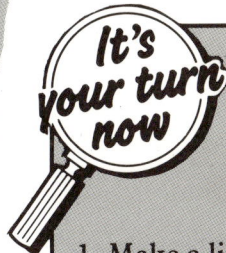

It's your turn now

During the war people didn't waste anything. Everything had to be re-used.

1 Make a list of all the things that were saved. Use Grandma's story to help you.

2 What do you think these things were used for after they'd been collected?

4 Invasion ... from London

The day Grandma waved goodbye to all her friends. Afterwards her school was shut down.

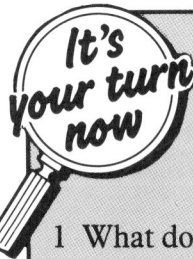

Matthew enjoyed hearing about Grandma's childhood but he didn't always understand her stories. Once she mentioned evacuation. He didn't know what that was, so he asked her on his next visit.

"Well, of course, I was never evacuated," said Grandma. "My mother wouldn't let me go." Then Grandma started to tell Matthew of the day she waved goodbye to all her friends. But Matthew still looked puzzled.

"I'm sorry, Grandma," he said. "I still don't understand. Why did you stay when your friends had to go away?"

It's your turn now

The pictures on these pages will help you to answer Matthew's question and these questions:

1 What does the word "evacuation" mean?

2 Why was it important to evacuate children?

3 What other groups do you think might have been evacuated?

were so cold. There was only cold water to wash in – and cold food, like bread and apples – and there weren't enough blankets for night-time. Some of them were crying and my mother got upset and that's why she kept me at home. Mum gave one girl my coat because she was so cold. I still remember her thanking us. Her accent was very strange – it was difficult to understand her."

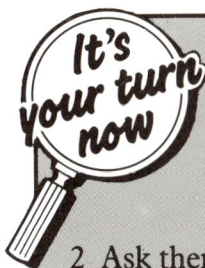

"Well," said Grandma, "when London children were first evacuated, some came to Great Yarmouth. They stayed in my school for a few nights before they went on to the villages. My mother said that when they arrived they were singing and laughing, but a lot soon became homesick. That was partly because they

It's your turn now

Grandma was not evacuated but many children were.

1 Do you know anyone who was evacuated?

2 Ask them what they remember. Was it fun, like a school trip? Or was it frightening, leaving their parents and going to live with strangers?

Great Yarmouth after a bombing raid. Do you think Grandma should have been evacuated with her friends?

5 Dad goes missing

George Ballard, Grandma's father. This was how Grandma remembered him – without his moustache!

At first, Dad going away didn't seem too bad. He was training with the Royal Air Force so he often came home. But then he stayed away longer and my mother became more worried. I realised afterwards that he was flying on bombing raids.

Matthew listened to Grandma's memories of evacuation but he was still puzzled about one thing. "Why did you hate the war, Grandma?" he asked. "It all sounds like fun – collecting things and no school!"

"I suppose I've tried to forget the unpleasant things," said Grandma. "And now it's difficult to remember exactly how I did feel. After all, it was a long time ago and I was only a child. But I *do* remember the worst part. That was missing my father. Even now I hate saying goodbye at the station.

Join the men who are hitting HARD!

Night and day Air Crews of the Royal Air Force are hitting the enemy on his own ground—and hitting him HARD. There is a chance for YOU to do a vital job with one of these crews — as Pilot, Observer or Wireless Operator/Air Gunner. If you are between 18 and 32 (even though you may already have registered for one of the Services) you can still volunteer for flying duties in the R.A.F.

Volunteer now—*and help to keep the R.A.F. supreme!*

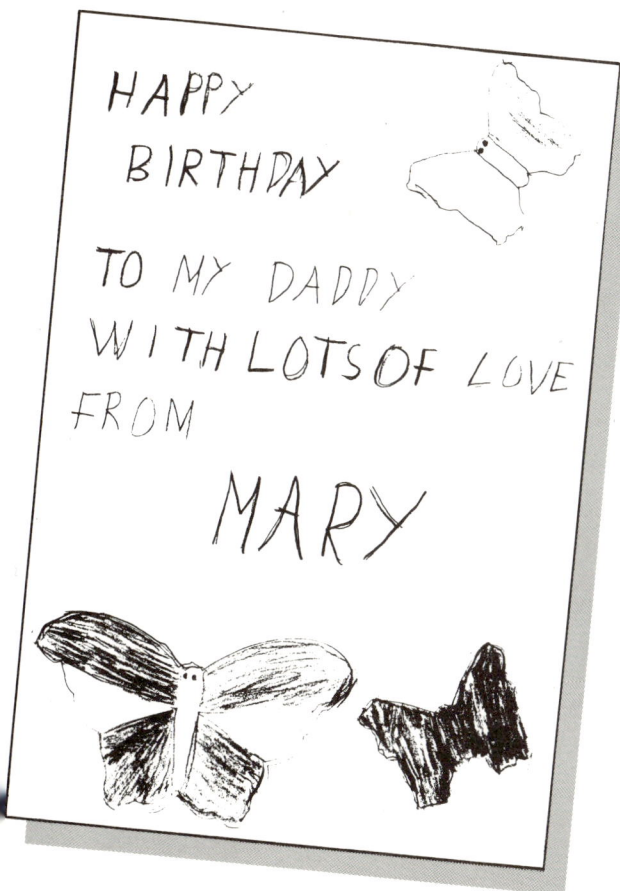

HAPPY BIRTHDAY
TO MY DADDY
WITH LOTS OF LOVE
FROM
MARY

When he did come home I hardly recognised him. He'd grown a moustache and looked quite different. And each visit went too quickly. Soon it was time to say goodbye. He told me to be brave but I remember my mother and I left the station crying.

The day the telegram came was the worst. My mother started crying and wouldn't tell me why. Then a neighbour took me to the park. Later they told me that my father was missing – his plane had crashed – but I didn't understand it clearly. For weeks afterwards, my mother wouldn't eat properly. All she seemed to do was work and work – she was always busy. She helped people who'd been bombed out, she worked at the canteen and she went round from door to door collecting blankets and things.

Some time later, a Red Cross worker came to the house and said that my father was a prisoner-of-war in Germany. It didn't bring him home but my mother was happier, knowing that he was safe. We were able to make up parcels for him – socks, chocolate, cigarettes, soap, things like that. And I used to make him Christmas cards, Easter cards, birthday cards, cards for everything.

It was a long time before he came home. And when he did, he'd changed so much. It was difficult getting to know him again.

The bomber crew

Many people had this kind of shelter in their gardens. They spent the night with candles, sandwiches, blankets and a flask of tea.

I missed my father most at night. There were heavy bombing raids and we had to sleep in shelters. We always went round to Grandad's. It was safer away from the gasworks and it gave my mother some company. But it wasn't the same without Dad.

One night we had a really big raid. First of all 'Moaning Minnie' started – that was what we called the warning siren. Then two big bombs dropped nearby. The ground was shaking and the air was full of smoke and dust.

It carried on all night. We could hear the droning noise of the bombers, then a whistling 'whoosh' as the bombs fell, then a crash like thunder as each bomb landed. For a long time afterwards I hated listening to the coalman dropping coal into our cellar. It reminded me of those terrible nights.

There were other sounds too that night – breaking glass, people shouting, dogs barking, whistles, hooters. There was a baby crying nearby, too, I remember that clearly. And all the time the planes kept droning on and on, overhead. I thought it would never end.

After the raid was over!

These people had no water at home because of the damage caused by bombing raids.

In the morning we walked back to our house. Everywhere we looked we saw damaged houses. Some fires were still smouldering. Our house wasn't too bad. The windows were all broken and one of the ceilings had fallen in. But the water and gas were cut off. We got our meals from a canteen at the end of the road and water from a standpipe. For days afterwards everything seemed to smell of smoke and taste of dust.

Oh yes, I hated the war then. It took my father away. I hated the war – those bombers and their pilots."

Matthew was very quiet while Grandma was talking. She seemed to have been very frightened and lonely during the war and he could see now why she hated it. But one thing still puzzled him. "Did you ever see any Germans, Grandma?" he asked.

"I did once," she answered slowly. "A fighter plane crashed off the coast and the lifeboat rescued the pilot. It was strange really – I was standing with a crowd on the quay and someone was jeering and booing. But when I saw the pilot close to, he looked just like Dad. He even had a moustache. I remember hoping that no one had booed my father when he was captured."

6 Keep it dark!

the material over the windows like big curtains, and at the front door Dad hung a blanket from a long pole. I suppose it was useful – it kept out the cold. But if the smallest chink of light showed outside, the warden banged on the door and shouted at us. 'Keep it dark' was the motto. It was a real change when the war ended. Everyone turned on their lights and someone lit a bonfire, just to brighten up the street."

Grandma enjoyed talking about her childhood and showing Matthew her treasures. They started to make a scrapbook, so Grandma asked her family and friends if Matthew could borrow their wartime mementoes.

Cousin Annie sent Grandma a bulky envelope full of photographs and newspaper cuttings. One showed people buying blackout material. "Oh, one shilling a yard," said Grandma, laughing. (That's about 5 pence a metre.) "It seems so cheap now, but my mother thought it was very expensive. I remember trailing from shop to shop trying to find thick, dark cloth. It was difficult getting any at all – everyone in town needed some.

The blackout became a way of life. It stayed until the war ended. We pinned

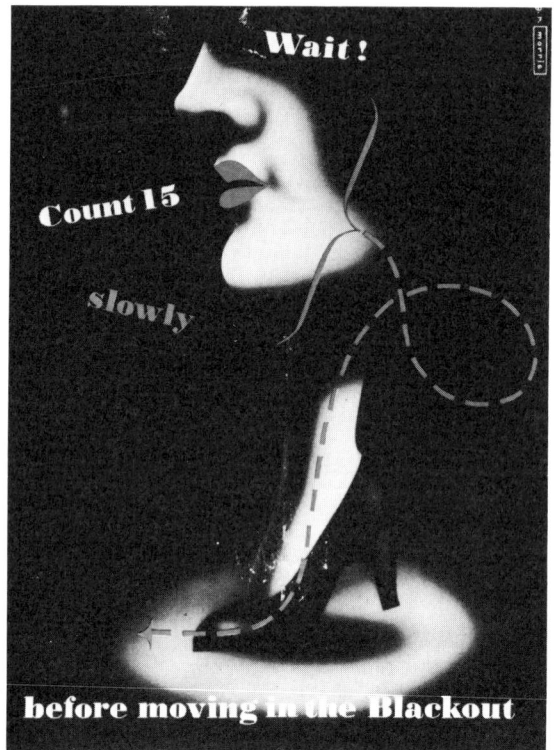

A poster from the Royal Society for the Prevention of Accidents. Why did people need to "wait and count 15 slowly before moving"?

It's your turn now

1 Grandma told Matthew that it was important to black out the lights. Why was it so important to stop light from showing outside?

2 The picture above shows a street as it would have looked during the blackout. It shows that people didn't only black out light from houses. Can you see any other things that were darkened?

3 Surprisingly, some things were made brighter instead of darker. Can you see any examples of this?

4 Why do you think some things were made brighter?

5 You can see how different the streets were in the blackout. Can you describe how you might have felt walking along the street shown in the picture?

6 What problems do you think you might have had walking along the street in the blackout?

7 Not carrots again, Mum!

Robert and Annie on their wedding day in 1944

Cousin Annie's parcel also contained a wedding photograph. This reminded Grandma of another big change that was caused by the war. "Annie and Robert got married when rationing was on," she said. "But their cake looked so fancy, covered in icing. We thought they must have saved up all their coupons and bought every bag of sugar in town. Then when we looked closely, it turned out to be a cardboard model. Inside, it was a plain, dark fruit cake – and it was made with dried eggs, prunes and carrots!"

Matthew remembered that Grandma had kept a ration book so he hunted through the sideboard until he found it.

DIG FOR VICTORY

"Where's my Weetabix?"

Sorry, dickybird, but nowadays we can't afford to throw away a single crumb of Weetabix. You see, the nourishment in Weetabix means so much more to us than to you. It means health and it means energy. And as we've been told to use it—as many other foods—sparingly; well, we've just got to make the most of every crumb.

Weetabix makes the most of wheat. You make the most of Weetabix. Here is a delightful change from the ordinary:—

WEETABIX AND BEAN SALAD (To serve 4 people)
3 Weetabix.
½ lb. cooked haricot beans.
1 oz. grated cheese.
Cream salad dressing.
Lettuce or watercress.
A few pickled onions or shallots.

Break Weetabix into small pieces, mix with cooked haricot beans and chopped onions. Line dish with lettuce leaves or watercress, pile vegetables in centre. Top with several spoonfuls thick salad dressing, sprinkle with cheese (finely grated).

Not only a most delicious savoury, but really a meal in itself.

Weetabix

Standard Size 7½d.
Double Size 1/1d.

More Weetabix is being made. If at times it is difficult to obtain, this is because more people are buying it.
Weetabix Ltd., Weetabix Mills, Burton Latimer, Northants

The Missing Link

OXO

LET OXO MEAT YOUR VEGETABLES

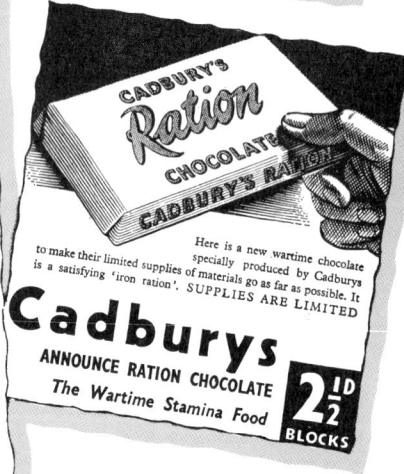

CADBURY'S Ration CHOCOLATE
CADBURY'S RATION

Here is a new wartime chocolate specially produced by Cadburys to make their limited supplies of materials go as far as possible. It is a satisfying 'iron ration'. SUPPLIES ARE LIMITED

Cadburys
ANNOUNCE RATION CHOCOLATE
The Wartime Stamina Food

2½d. BLOCKS

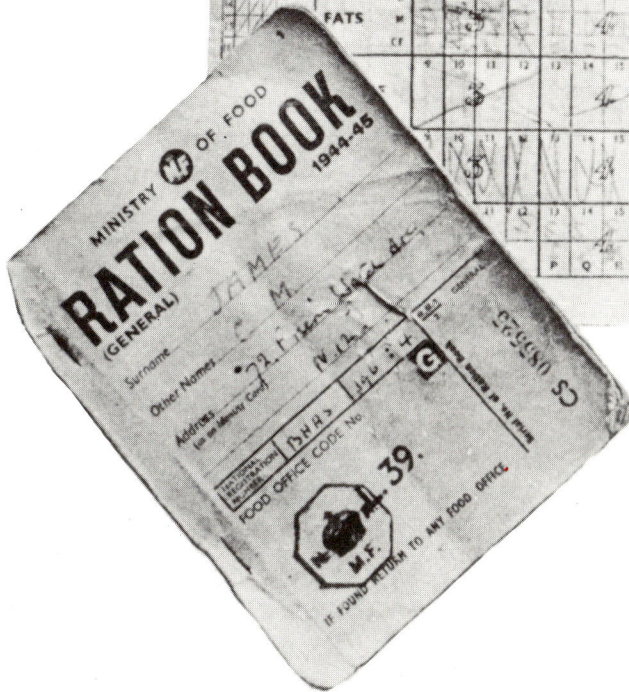

we did have plenty of carrots. If I wasn't eating them I was growing them or scrubbing them.

But young John was worse off. He had to have cod liver oil for the vitamins. It tasted horrid. And it made him smell all fishy."

He also found some meat coupons and a lot of food advertisements in an old magazine. But a recipe for Weetabix with haricot beans and onions made him turn his nose up. "Did you really eat this, Grandma?" he asked. "Wasn't there any meat to go with the onions?"

"There's no need to pull that face," replied Grandma. "The meals weren't all so awful. But some were a bit strange, like the banana sandwiches. Years later I discovered they never had banana in them at all. It was parsnips mashed with banana essence.

There were shortages, too. My mother used to make her arms ache shaking up the top of the milk for extra butter. But

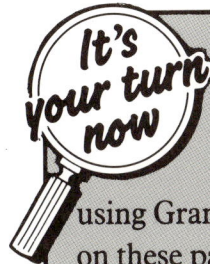

It's your turn now

Matthew asked Grandma a lot of questions about food rationing. Can you answer each of these four questions using Grandma's story and the pictures on these pages to help you? Are there any other questions you would like to ask about food rationing?

1 Why was food rationed?

2 What sorts of foods were rationed?

3 Could people do anything to help themselves?

4 Did children get anything special?

8 Make do and mend

"Of course food wasn't the only thing that was rationed," said Grandma. "Petrol, coal, shoes and clothing were rationed as well." Grandma handed Matthew a family photograph. "That christening took place a few years after the war ended, but the clothes still make it look like wartime. No frills or fancies. 'Make do and mend' was the motto. Everything had to be sensible and serviceable.

I remember my grandad grumbling about a new suit. To save cloth, the trousers didn't have turn-ups and the jacket didn't have enough pockets for everything he carried. Then he found that his shirt was so short he couldn't tuck it in properly.

But I think the rationing was worst for us children. We were growing so quickly we always needed bigger clothes. Luckily my mother was good at sewing and she used up every scrap of material. John's vests were made from new dusters and his trousers from blackout cloth. Even so, we didn't have a lot of clothes like you and Nicola. I just had two dresses. One to wear and one in the wash.

I can still remember my tenth birthday. My mother had saved six coupons. They were my present. It was a real treat deciding what to get. Guess what I chose?"

It's your turn now

The pictures below show how many coupons you would need to exchange when buying new clothes.

1 What clothes could Grandma have chosen with her six coupons?

2 If you had six coupons, what would you choose?

ISSUED BY THE BOARD OF TRADE

"Look what Mummy's done with my old overcoat"

8 coupons saved

Any boy would be proud to wear a snug Battle Blouse like this. And many mothers will be thankful for the hint on how to make an outgrown overcoat do for another season. The idea came from a Make-do and Mend class—why not visit one and get help with your own sewing problems?

The old coat was cut short just below the waist—that gave material for cuff bands, belt and pockets.

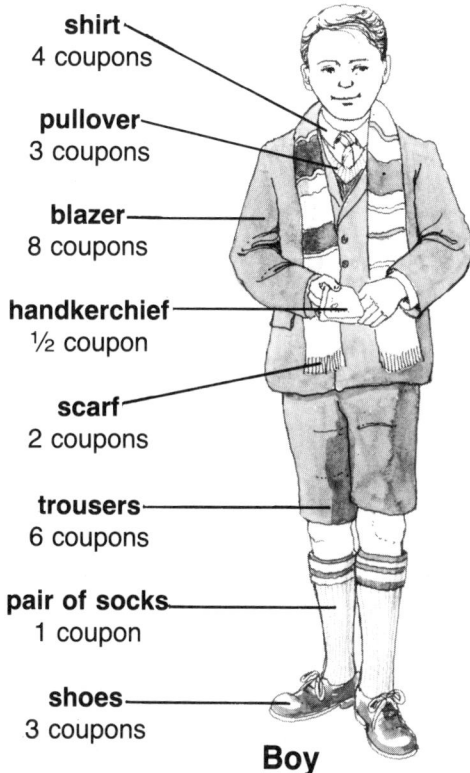

shirt
4 coupons

pullover
3 coupons

blazer
8 coupons

handkerchief
½ coupon

scarf
2 coupons

trousers
6 coupons

pair of socks
1 coupon

shoes
3 coupons

Boy

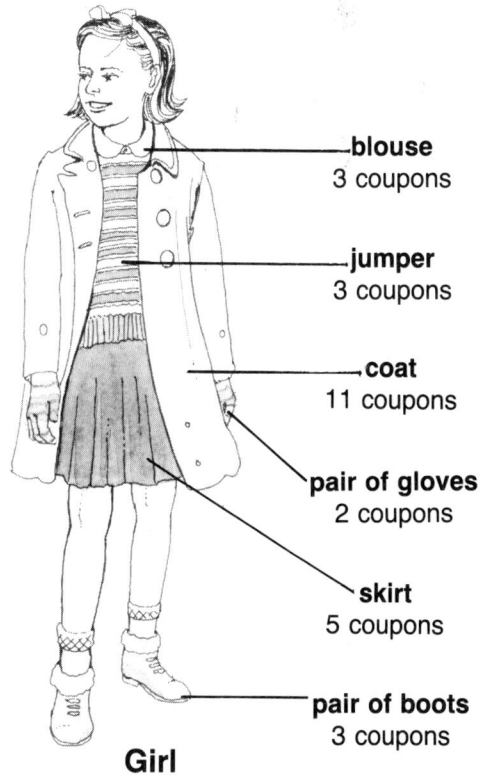

blouse
3 coupons

jumper
3 coupons

coat
11 coupons

pair of gloves
2 coupons

skirt
5 coupons

pair of boots
3 coupons

Girl

9 Too old to fly

"I would have been a pilot," said Matthew as he was sticking pictures in his scrapbook. "I've read all about flying. It's exciting and full of adventures."

"But I don't think it was really like that," replied Grandma. "My father said that wartime flying was always cold and sometimes very frightening. Anyway," she added, "some people couldn't join the fighting forces. They were told they had to stay at home doing important jobs like farming and mining.

Do you remember that christening photo, Matthew? Only one of the young men was in the forces – he was a soldier.

The "old chap" in Home Guard uniform with his daughter.

Home Guard soldiers capture "an enemy" – everybody took their turn to be a German soldier.

A lesson for the Home Guard – how to defuse bombs.

Members of the WVS helping the war effort.

One of the others was with the railways and one worked for an oil company. And it was the same for the women in that picture. One was in the women's army, one was in the police and the other was a nurse."

"Well, I bet the old chap at the back took it easy," said Matthew cheekily. "He was too old to fly."

"And that's where you're wrong," replied Grandma. "He probably had the most tiring job of all. During the day he worked in a weapons factory and in his spare time he was a Home Guard. He did his bit to win the war."

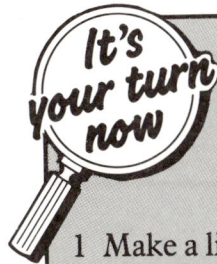

It's your turn now

There were many ways of helping to win the war. Some jobs were full-time and some were part-time.

1 Make a list of wartime jobs. You can use Grandma's story and the pictures in the book to help you. You might also find some clues on earlier pages.

2 While men joined the Home Guard, many women joined the Women's Voluntary Service (WVS). What sorts of jobs did people in the Home Guard or the WVS do? There is some information on these pages to help answer this question but you may be able to find out more by talking to your family and their friends.

10 Matthew Barlow, Time Detective

Matthew's scrapbook – A family in the war.

Matthew enjoyed finding out about Grandma's family in the war. He put the pictures and cuttings they collected in his scrapbook and he wrote down Grandma's stories. He found out a lot that he hadn't known before.

"It's a bit like being a detective," Matthew said to Grandma one afternoon. "You know, finding clues about people, then using the clues as evidence. I've been able to work out all sorts of things – what people did and why."

"Yes," replied Grandma, "except that detectives solve today's mysteries. You're working out what happened forty years ago. That makes you a Time Detective!"

It's your turn now

On the opposite page you can see some of the evidence that Matthew found.

1 Can you find four different *types* of evidence and fill them in on the chart ?

2 Which of the four types of evidence was the most helpful for Matthew?

3 Grandma told Matthew a lot about the war. Why did Matthew need to look for more evidence?

4 Could Matthew have found out about the war without any evidence?

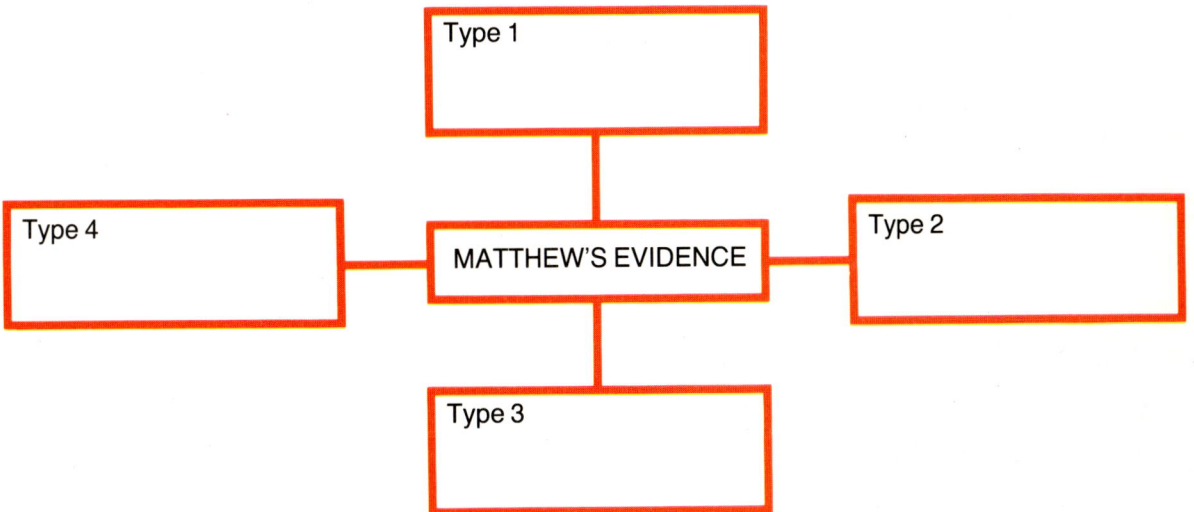

Type 1

Type 4

MATTHEW'S EVIDENCE

Type 2

Type 3

11 All change!

While he was listening to Grandma's stories, Matthew found out more and more about the war. He also found out another reason why Grandma had hated it. As a little girl, she had wanted everything to stay the same but then the war had started. Whatever Matthew looked at, Grandma said it had been changed by the war.

Sorry I can't play dominoes tonight – it's my turn to be fire watching.

I hope he'll come back soon.

CHANGES IN A LITTLE GIRL'S LIFE

We'd better get the blackout curtains up before it gets dark.

Why don't we have bananas any more?

NATIONAL REGISTRATION IDENTITY CARD

Hitler will send no warning —
so always carry your gas mask

ISSUED BY THE MINISTRY OF HOME SECURITY

I wonder who'll play with me now.

I'm sorry I couldn't wrap it.

It's your turn now

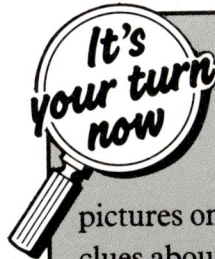

The war changed everyone's life. Some of the biggest changes happened as soon as the war started. The pictures on these pages give you some clues about these changes.

1 What changes do these clues tell you about?

2 Why were these changes made?

3 Do you think they made life easier or more difficult?

4 Can you find any evidence of other changes earlier in the book?

12 Poppy Day!

While they were shopping one day Grandma, Matthew and Nicky saw a lady with a tray of paper poppies. "Oh, she's collecting for Remembrance Day," said Grandma. "Here's some money for the tin."

"But what do we have to remember?" asked Matthew. Grandma smiled. She knew she had some explaining to do.

"We're remembering all the brave people who died in the wars," said Grandma. "I've been telling you about the war that happened when I was a child. Well, there was another war with Germany, years before I was born, when my mother was a child. *My* grandfather fought in that war – World War One we call it now.

When that war ended, people wanted a special day for remembering their friends and relatives who'd been killed. They chose 11th November as Remembrance Day because World War One ended at 11 o'clock on 11th November 1918. When I was a girl, everyone stood still at 11 o'clock and remembered those who'd been killed or injured. Trams stopped, men got off their bicycles, no one spoke – it was very sad and a bit eerie."

You will see war memorials in every town and village. They record the names of local people killed in both world wars.

Remembrance Day in 1926

"But why do we buy poppies?" asked Nicky.

"Well, I'm not sure," replied Grandma. "You'll have to ask Matthew to help you find out. He's getting quite good at being a detective!"

On the way home, Matthew asked Grandma more questions about World War One. "Was there food rationing? Did they have a blackout?"

Grandma couldn't answer him. "I remember things about World War Two," she said. "But World War One was fought before I was even born. So I can't tell you about it. I don't think we know anyone old enough who can tell us."

But then Grandma remembered she had an old suitcase full of her grandfather's things. "Perhaps we do have some clues after all," she said, "even if we've no one to talk to. If we're lucky we may find out about my grandfather, as well as World War One."

13 Almost another world

Grandfather Fred and his family in 1923.
Grandma's father is standing in the middle.

Frank, aged 14, photographed in 1902.

Opening the suitcase, Matthew found an old photograph album. The first picture showed a family sitting together. "Oh, look, that's my father as a boy," said Grandma. "Just look at that collar. And that's my grandfather, Fred. He was a soldier in World War One. I don't know much about my grandmother, though. Her family were farming people from Berkshire. My grandparents came to Yarmouth sometime after World War One."

The next picture showed Fred's younger brother, Frank, as a boy. "He was in the army all his life," said Grandma. "You remember him, Matthew. He was the old chap in the christening photo – the one in the Home Guard."

Then Matthew looked at some of Frank's army photographs from India. "Was it like this in England as well?" he asked. "Did everyone use a horse and cart in the old days? It looks very slow!"

This made Grandma laugh. "A lot of people did," she said. "This rushing about in cars and planes is something new. Things have changed since I was a girl. We used bicycles or the tram. And I think things have changed even more

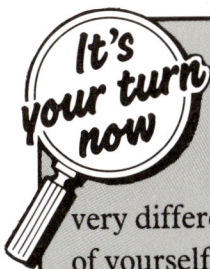

It's your turn now

These pages show some photographs that were taken between about 1900 and 1920. They probably look very different from photographs you have of yourself and your family.

1 Look at the pictures of Matthew's family. Make a list of which things have changed and which have stayed the same.

2 This page also shows two cars which are very different from ones you see today. Can you think of other things which have changed? Try to find pictures to show what they looked like in about 1910.

since my mother was a girl." And to show Matthew what she meant, Grandma opened the encyclopaedia at the section on motor cars.

The "Bullnose" Morris Oxford, 1912 – this was the kind of car on the road when Grandma's mother was a girl. Only the rich could afford cars.

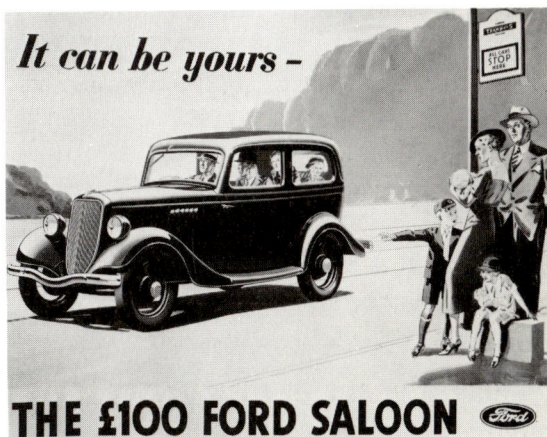

It can be yours –

THE £100 FORD SALOON *Ford*

A Ford Popular, made in 1935 – Grandma saw these cars every day when she was a girl but only one person in her road had one.

14 Fred joins the army

Fred (on the right) at training camp after he'd joined up in 1916.

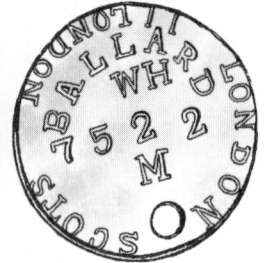

A sketch of the disc Fred wore round his neck to show his identity (above), and his cap badge (below).

The suitcase turned out to be a real treasure-chest. In an old envelope there was a bundle of army things. One of the pictures showed Fred, in soldier's uniform, standing with his friends. "Was your grandfather always a soldier?" Matthew asked Grandma.

"Only during World War One," she replied. "He gave up his job with the railway company and left his wife and children behind to go fighting in France."

This surprised Matthew – his mother always said that people were lucky to have good jobs. So he asked Grandma why Fred had been so keen to join the army.

"Well, I don't know for sure," replied Grandma, "and he isn't here to tell us. But we do have these letters and papers of his. They may give us some clues."

A telegram sent by Fred to his wife. He sent another telegram on 31st August 1916 saying "Today's the day".

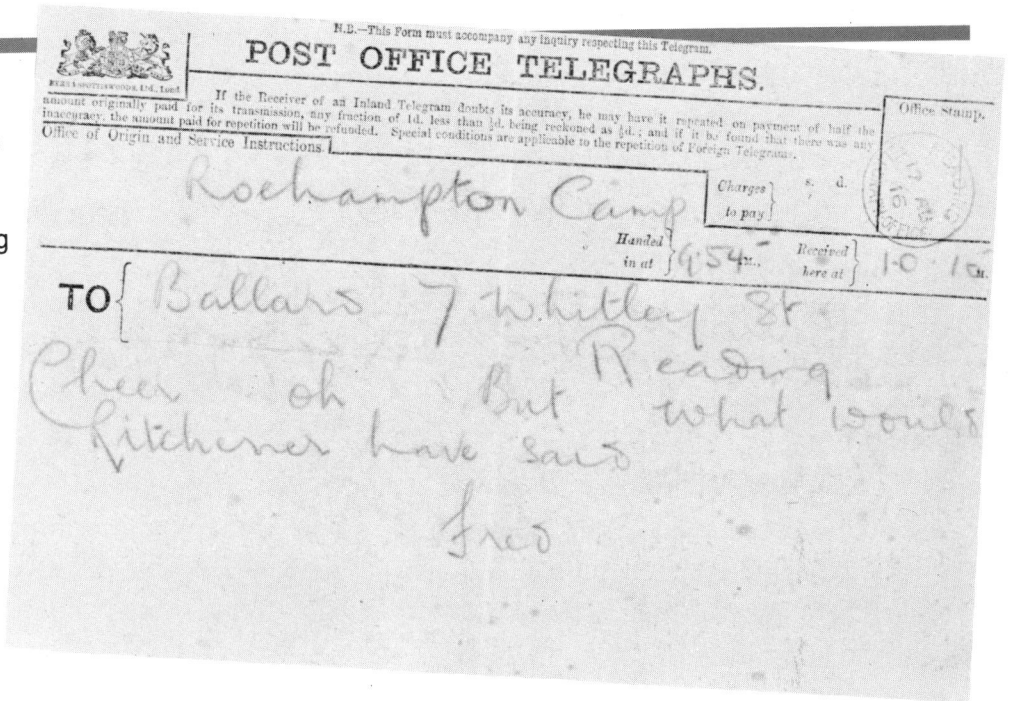

POST OFFICE TELEGRAPHS.

N.B.—This Form must accompany any inquiry respecting this Telegram.

If the Receiver of an Inland Telegram doubts its accuracy, he may have it repeated on payment of half the amount originally paid for its transmission, any fraction of 1d. less than ½d. being reckoned as ½d.; and if it be found that there was any inaccuracy, the amount paid for repetition will be refunded. Special conditions are applicable to the repetition of Foreign Telegrams.
Office of Origin and Service Instructions.

Rochampton Camp

TO Ballans 7 Whitley St
Cheer oh But Reading
Kitchener have said what would

Fred

Not all the clues were straightforward. At first Grandma found the telegram confusing. "What would Kitchener have said?" She knew that Kitchener was a famous general who encouraged *men* to join the army during World War One. But what did the telegram mean? Then she remembered that her Auntie Freda had been born on 16th August 1916. Can you work out what Auntie Freda's birth had to do with the telegram?

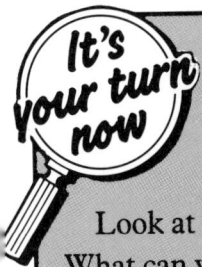

It's your turn now

As Grandma and Matthew looked through the envelope they learned about Fred, his family and his wartime life.

Look at the evidence on these pages. What can you find out about Fred and his family? There are also some clues on pages 28 and 29 and on the family tree on page 2.

BRITONS
"WANTS" YOU
JOIN YOUR COUNTRY'S ARMY!
GOD SAVE THE KING

Reproduced by permission of LONDON OPINION

Everyone knew this poster. Lord Kitchener was asking every fit young man to join the army.

15 Why the men joined up

Grandma and Matthew found out quite a lot about Fred but they didn't learn why he had given up his job to join the army. In fact, the more they found out about Fred the more it seemed a strange decision. When Fred went to France he left behind his wife, his son and a two-week-old daughter he probably hadn't seen. There were no clues in Fred's belongings to explain why he had volunteered.

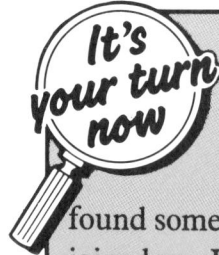

Matthew and Grandma went to the library and looked through some books on World War One. They found some clues, showing why men had joined up. Look at the clues on these pages. How many different reasons can you find for men joining the army?

Recruiting posters

Some women thought that men who had not joined the forces were cowards, and gave them white feathers.

A cartoon from *Punch* magazine, 9th September 1914

What happened to Fred?

10/10/16.

Dear Wynn,

I sent you a card this morning giving the address I am going on alright, it is only a bullet wound and will soon get better so there is nothing to worry about. I lost all my kit at the Somme so will you please send on my safety razor

as soon as possible also some money. No doubt you will have received this months cheque by now. Love to all from

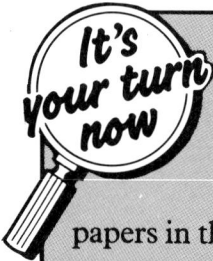

Fred.

It's your turn now

Grandma and Matthew discovered that Fred only stayed in France for a few months. The letters and papers in the suitcase showed that he came home suddenly and never returned to the trenches again. Can you work out what happened to Fred?

Form Z. 518.

CERTIFICATE OF EMPLOYMENT DURING THE WAR.

(To be completed for and handed to each airman.)

Every airman is advised to send a copy, rather than the original, when corresponding with a prospective employer.

It is particularly important that an apprentice whose apprenticeship has been interrupted by military service should have recorded on this Form any employment in a trade similar to his own in which he has been engaged during such military service.

No. 87893

Rank Lv. Leyt.

Names in full (surname first) Wallace: Welfred Jones

Unit. R.A.F. DETAILS PAY SECTION R.A.F. Trade Clerk

1. Employment in the R.A.F., R.N.A.S. or R.F.C.
   Trade.
   (a) Clerk. From Ap.12/17. Period. Feb 28/19
   (b) .... " .... " ....
   (c) .... " .... " ....
   Employment in any unit of the Naval or Military Forces of the Crown.
   Trade. Period.
   (a) 14. London From Ap.8/16. To Ap.12/17
   (b) ....
   If an airman has re-mustered in the course of his service in the R.N.A.S., R.F.C. or R.A.F., the period of his working at each trade should be given.

2. Trade or calling before enlistment (as shown in A.B. 64).
   Clerk

3. (i) Courses of Instruction in the R.A.F., R.N.A.S. or R.F.C., and certificates, if any.
   (a) ....
   (b) ....
   (c) ....
   (ii) Courses of Instruction in the R.N. and certificates, if any.
   (a) ....
   (b) ....
   (iii) Army Courses of Instruction and Courses in Active Service Army Schools.
   (a) ....
   (b) ....

No. <s>4 OCT 1916</s>
(If replying, please quote above No.)

Army Form B. 104—81.

T.F. RECORD OFFICE
4, LONDON WALL BLDGS., E.C. _____ Record Office,
_____ Station.

Madame
~~Sir~~ 14 OCT 1916 , 191

I regret to have to inform you that a report has this day been received from the War Office to the effect that (No.) 7522

(Rank) Pte (Name) Ballard W H

*Strike out words that do not apply.

(Regiment) 1/ THE LONDON SCOTTISH

Gunshot Wound R. Forearm was {*dangerously / *severely / *slightly}

wounded in action and admitted 3 Scot. Hospl. Rouen

on the 7 day of Oct 1916.

I am at the same time to express the sympathy and regret of the Army Council.

Any further information received in this office as to his condition will be at once notified to you.

I am,
Madame
~~Sir~~

Your obedient Servant,

G F Bartlett Maj for COL

½ TERRITORIAL FORCE RECORD OFFICE

Officer in charge of Records.

(4 27 1) W 13081—273 400,000 3/15 H W V(P) Forms/B. 104—80/2

TO BE SENT TO THE NEXT OF KIN, TO WHOM IT WILL SERVE AS THE OFFICIAL NOTIFICATION.

(Army Form W. 3229.)

ON HIS MAJESTY'S SERVICE.

Ward 14 B.

I have just arrived at

3rd SCOTTISH GENERAL

hospital at

STOBHILL, GLASGOW.

(The name and place of the hospital are not to be filled in by the soldier.)

Name Pte W. H. Ballard

Regiment 14" London

Regtl. No. 7522

ADDRESS.

OFFICIAL PAID

Mrs Ballard
7 Whitley Street
Reading.

17 Soldier Fred's feelings

Stobhill Hospital
November 1916

Dear Wynn,
    I am sorry that my leave with you and the children went badly. It wasn't your fault. I couldn't abide all those people talking about revenge, just because of this wound. They don't seem to understand anything about the fighting. There's not many of us who really hate old Jerry. At least Jerry knows what it's like to live in wet and muddy trenches.

    I got fed up with the newspapers too. I know they're trying to keep up our spirits – but they make it all seem exciting and successful. They say we're all heroes – but when there was a raid on I felt lonely and frightened. They never print that in the newspaper.

    Sorry to moan on. I hope things will be easier next time.
        Love to all,
        Fred

It's your turn now

Matthew was surprised by the letter. The stories in his comics made war seem exciting but Fred didn't seem at all excited. Fred said that life in the trenches was wet, muddy and frightening.

1 Look at the photographs on the opposite page. Do they support Fred's view? Try to give reasons for your answer.

2 Why do you think the newspapers wanted to make the fighting seem exciting and successful?

3 How did the people at home expect Fred to feel about the enemy after he was wounded?

4 How did Fred's feelings about "old Jerry" differ from those of the people at home?

5 Can you explain why Fred felt differently?

TOMMY (finding a German prisoner who speaks English): "Look what you done to me, you blighters! 'Ere—'ave a cigarette?"

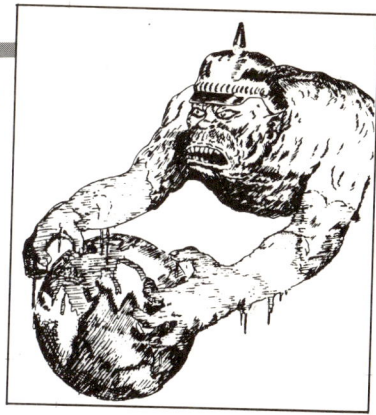

1 *A Punch* cartoon, published in 1915.

2 A newspaper cartoon. How would it make people in England feel about Germany?

3 British soldiers helping German wounded in 1917.

4 Stretcher bearers struggling through the mud.

18 The enemy goes down

"We've been lucky to find out so much about Fred," said Grandma. "But we don't know nearly as much about his brothers. We've got those pictures of Frank but we don't even know what the older brother, Harry, looked like. Do those letters tell us anything about him?"

"Well, there's this," replied Matthew, "but it's difficult to understand."

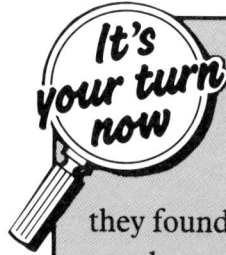

It's your turn now

Quite a few things in the letter puzzled Matthew. So Grandma and Matthew went down to the library where they found these clues in a book. Can you use these clues to help you answer each of Matthew's four questions?

1 What did Harry do in World War One?

2 What were the *Blücher* and the *Tiger*?

3 What happened to Scarborough?

4 Why did Harry feel sorry for the German sailors at the end of the letter?

My dear Emily,

I'm writing to let you know that I'm safe and well. Our scrap caused a few casualties on Tiger but we're all keen to have another go.

We caught their fleet sneaking towards poor old Scarboro' again. But we got our revenge on the Blücher and sent the rest packing. They got their come-uppance. Perhaps they'll think twice before threatening our women again.

The German survivors looked a sorry sight. Not exactly the pride of their navy — just wet and bedraggled. I'm glad I wasn't in their shoes. But they were the lucky ones — a lot of the men on the Blücher drowned.

There's no news yet of leave. I'll send a telegram as soon as I know.

My regards to your family,

Your dearest friend,
Harry

The *Blücher* sinking. You can see men jumping into the sea but only 200 survived. Almost 800 sailors were drowned.

MEN OF BRITAIN!
WILL YOU STAND THIS?

No 2 Wykeham Street, SCARBOROUGH, after the German bombardment on Dec! 16th. It was the Home of a Working Man. Four People were killed in this House including the Wife aged 58, and Two Children, the youngest aged 5.

78 Women & Children were killed and 228 Women & Children were wounded by the German Raiders
ENLIST NOW

There was little bombing in World War One. How did people react to attacks on Scarborough by the German navy?

But there was one mystery they couldn't solve. Who was Emily? "I don't remember anyone in the family talking about an Emily," said Grandma. "I wonder who she was? And how did her letter get back to Fred?"

19 The enemy ... next door

A mob looting a German-owned shop in London in 1915.

Camps had to be built quickly to take all the foreigners who were imprisoned. This picture shows a camp in the middle of a racecourse.

"I wish your grandfather was still alive," said Matthew one afternoon. "Then he could do some explaining for me. It seems that both Fred and Harry hated Germany for starting the war. But they didn't hate the German people they saw – the ordinary soldiers and sailors. Do you understand that, Grandma?"

"Well, I'm not sure," replied Grandma. "Even now I wouldn't want to go to Germany."

"But you did feel a bit sorry for that pilot they rescued from the sea," interrupted Matthew. "Did you ever feel like that about any other German person?"

"There was someone else," replied Grandma slowly. "When I was a child we lived in the same street as a family called Müller. She was English but he was a German fisherman. We didn't hate him. He was just one of the neighbours.

Mr Müller was often ill so my mother helped with their shopping. For years he kept quiet about his illness but in the end we found out, by chance. After we'd been on holiday to the Isle of Man, Mr Müller told me that he'd been in prison there.

German and other foreigners being marched to prison. Why were they so well guarded?

He told me that at the beginning of World War One the newspapers were full of spy stories. Everyone with a foreign-sounding name was suspected of spying. So all the Germans living here were arrested and locked in dirty, cold prison camps. In the meantime, their families had to make do with little money or food.

By the time Mr Müller was released, he was a different person – old, tired and sometimes grumpy. But even so, we didn't hate him. He always made the time to talk to us children."

Suddenly the old clock on the mantelpiece chimed 5 o'clock. "Is that the time?" said Grandma. "I don't know where the minutes go – helping you with that scrapbook, I expect. How on earth did all this start?"

"Well, it started with me telling you about my holiday friends from Germany," said Matthew. "Perhaps you would have liked them after all. Even Fred and Harry might have understood about me having German friends."

Matthew, Nicky and their German friend, Benz, on holiday. "Even Fred and Harry might have understood about me having German friends."

20 Feelings ... and reasons

Matthew enjoyed searching through Grandma's family treasures. He found out what his relatives did in the wars. And he began to learn about Grandma's feelings and the feelings of his relatives, even though this wasn't so easy.

When Matthew and Grandma started finding out about the two wars, Grandma said she wouldn't have anything to do with German people. This was because of the war when she was a little girl. But later on she started to change her mind.

She still hated the war and she hated the German leaders for starting it. But now she didn't think it was fair to blame all the German people, particularly young children like Matthew and Nicky's friends.

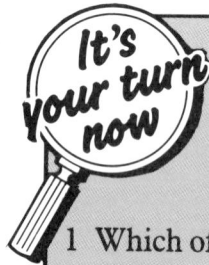

It's your turn now

The pictures below show some things that affected Grandma's attitude to Germany and the war.

1 Which of them made Grandma hate the war?

2 Which of them changed Grandma's mind about ordinary German people?

Matthew didn't just find out what people did or how they felt. He also tried to find out their reasons for doing things.

This wasn't always easy. People's reasons are often very complicated. They can have different ideas or wishes at the same time. For example, there have probably been times when *you* weren't sure what you wanted to do most – a time when you wanted to stay in and watch a TV programme but you also wanted to go out and play with your friends.

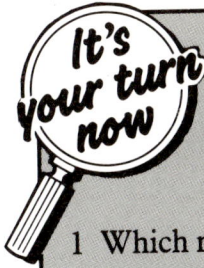

It's your turn now

Matthew found that Fred had mixed feelings about joining the army. Look at the pictures below.

1 Which reasons made Fred want to join the army?

2 Which reasons made him want to stay at home?

That's my last football game – I'll be in the army next week.

YOUR COUNTRY NEEDS YOU

Think twice about joining up, Fred, you've got a good safe job here.

21 Matthew – Time Detective

This book has followed Matthew's investigations as a
Time Detective. Below is a chart showing the different
things Matthew found out about his family.

Matthew looked for
EVIDENCE
about his family

He used the evidence
to find out about
their lives in the wars

Their
MOTIVES

Their
FEELINGS

The CHANGES
in their lives

and ...

Grandma said that Matthew was a kind of Time Detective. If he had been older she would probably have called him by a different name. What else could we call Matthew?

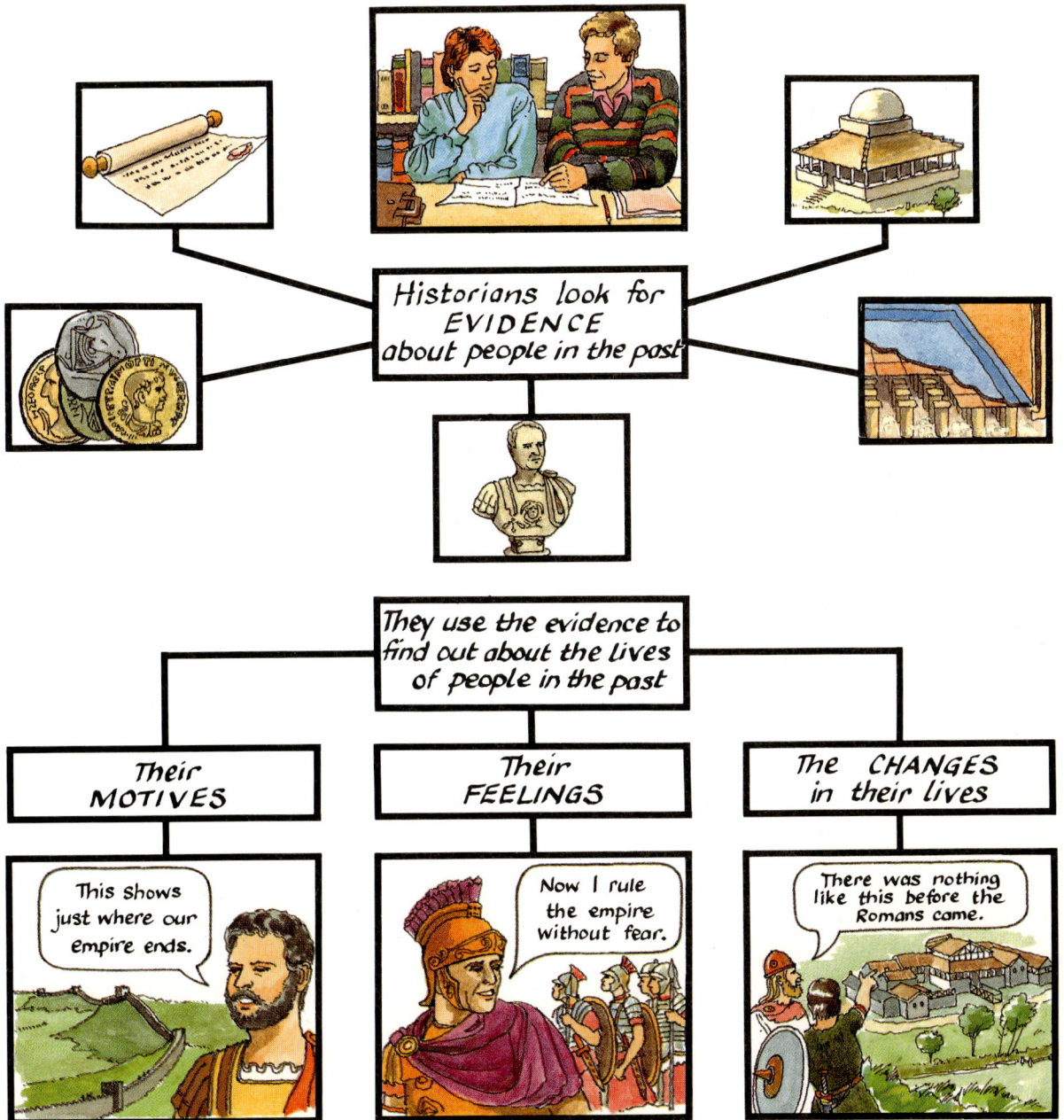

Historians look for EVIDENCE about people in the past

They use the evidence to find out about the lives of people in the past

Their MOTIVES	Their FEELINGS	The CHANGES in their lives

This shows just where our empire ends.

Now I rule the empire without fear.

There was nothing like this before the Romans came.

22 Investigating your family

Throughout this book you have been reading about Matthew's search for his family history. But you could investigate your own family's wartime lives by following in Matthew's footsteps.

The picture strip suggests how you might become your own family's historian. But don't be disappointed if you can't find as many sources as Matthew did – he was very lucky!

Do your parents or grandparents have any wartime memories or records?

Do any other relatives have evidence about your family in wartime?

Check in library books to find out about events which affected your family.

Museums also give information about these events.

And while you're working . . . . keep a record of all your discoveries for younger relatives.

If you do start finding out about your family in wartime you'll probably learn a lot about the two world wars. Some of your own family might have fought a long way from home. All over the world soldiers, sailors and airmen did many brave deeds. At home people were just as brave. They coped with being bombed and worked to support the fighting forces.

All these people were members of families – your parents, grandparents and great-grandparents. They were the heroes and heroines of wartime for you to find out about.

1 Sikh soldiers in World War One
2 "War in the Far East"
3 Women heaving coal
4 The Allied invasion of France
5 V.E. Day
6 Desert warfare

Acknowledgements

The author and publishers wish to acknowledge the following photograph sources:

Barnaby's Picture Library, page 12 (top left); BBC Hulton Picture Library, pages 7 (right), 8, 11 (right), 12 (top right), 13 (top), 13 (bottom), 14 (left), 21 (middle), 25 (left), 26/27, 33 (bottom), 40 (top); British Motor Industry Heritage Trust, page 29 (bottom left); Brooke Bond Oxo Ltd, page 16; Cadbury Ltd, page 16; J. Allan Cash Ltd, page 27 (bottom left); Ford Motor Company Ltd, page 29 (bottom right); Imperial War Museum, pages 9 (top), 14 (top right), 16, 20 (bottom), 21 (top), 21 (bottom), 25 (middle), 25 (right), 31 (bottom), 32 (left), 32 (middle), 39 (bottom), 47 (centre left), 47 (centre middle), 47 (bottom left), 47 (bottom right); IPC Magazines Ltd, page 4 (top), 5 (top left), 19; Mail Newspapers plc, page 39 (top); Popperfoto, page 47 (centre right); Royal British Legion, Page 26; Weetabix Ltd, page 16.

Cover photograph Topham Picture Library

The publishers have made every effort to trace all the copyright holders, but where they have failed to do so they will be pleased to make the necessary arrangements at the first opportunity.

First published 1988
Reprinted 1990

Published by
MACMILLAN EDUCATION LTD
Houndmills, Basingstoke, Hampshire RG21 2XS
and London
Companies and representatives
throughout the world

Illustrated by Chris Evans
Cover illustration Norma Burgin
Designed by Sylvia Tate

Printed in Hong Kong

British Library Cataloguing in Publication Data
Dawson, Ian and Pat,
A family in the wars.—(Time Detectives).
1. World War, 1914-1918—Great Britain
2. Great Britain—Social life and customs—20th century
3. World War, 1939-1945—Great Britain
4. Great Britain—Social life and customs—20th century.
I. Title   II. Series
941.083   DA566.4
ISBN 0–333–38842–9